Happiness radiates like the fragrance from a flower and draws all good things towards you.

Maharishi Mahesh Yogi

Pug in a Rug Journal

Pug in a Rug Journal

Pug in a Rug Journal

Pug in a Rug Journal

If you believe in yourself and have dedication and pride - and never quit, you'll be a winner. The price of victory is high but so are the rewards.

Paul Bryant

Pug in a Rug Journal

Pug in a Rug Journal

Pug in a Rug Journal

Pug in a Rug Journal

Inspiration comes from within yourself. One has to be positive. When you're positive, good things happen.

Deep Roy

Pug in a Rug Journal

Pug in a Rug Journal

Pug in a Rug Journal

Pug in a Rug Journal

Things turn out best for the people who make the best of the way things turn out.

John Wooden

Pug in a Rug Journal

Pug in a Rug Journal

Pug in a Rug Journal

Pug in a Rug Journal

Learn from yesterday, live for today, hope for tomorrow. The important thing is not to stop questioning.

Albert Einstein

Pug in a Rug Journal

Pug in a Rug Journal

Pug in a Rug Journal

Pug in a Rug Journal

Hope is the only bee that makes honey without flowers.

Robert Green Ingersoll

Pug in a Rug Journal

Pug in a Rug Journal

Pug in a Rug Journal

Pug in a Rug Journal

Believe in yourself, and the rest will fall into place. Have faith in your own abilities, work hard, and there is nothing you cannot accomplish.

Brad Henry

Pug in a Rug Journal

Pug in a Rug Journal

Pug in a Rug Journal

Pug in a Rug Journal

Once you replace negative thoughts with positive ones, you'll start having positive results.

Willie Nelson

Pug in a Rug Journal

Pug in a Rug Journal

Pug in a Rug Journal

Pug in a Rug Journal

Good things happen to those who hustle.

Chuck Noll

Pug in a Rug Journal

Pug in a Rug Journal

Pug in a Rug Journal

Pug in a Rug Journal

In order to carry a positive action we must develop here a positive vision.

Dalai Lama

Pug in a Rug Journal

Pug in a Rug Journal

Pug in a Rug Journal

Pug in a Rug Journal

All human wisdom is summed up in two words; wait and hope.

Alexandre Dumas

Pug in a Rug Journal

Pug in a Rug Journal

Pug in a Rug Journal

Pug in a Rug Journal

Believe in love. Believe in magic. Hell, believe in Santa Clause. Believe in others. Believe in yourself. Believe in your dreams. If you don't, who will?

Jon Bon Jovi

Pug in a Rug Journal

Pug in a Rug Journal

Pug in a Rug Journal

Pug in a Rug Journal

There is hope in dreams, imagination, and in the courage of those who wish to make those dreams a reality.

Jonas Salk

Pug in a Rug Journal

Pug in a Rug Journal

Pug in a Rug Journal

Pug in a Rug Journal

You just have to believe in yourself when you've got something, and just keep pounding on the door, because if you pound long enough, somebody is going to open it.

Cynthia Weil

Pug in a Rug Journal

Pug in a Rug Journal

Pug in a Rug Journal

Pug in a Rug Journal

When you think positive, good things happen.

Matt Kemp

Pug in a Rug Journal

Pug in a Rug Journal

Pug in a Rug Journal

Pug in a Rug Journal

Everything's very perfectly balanced; for all the horrible things in the world there's lots of good things.

John Frusciante

Pug in a Rug Journal

Pug in a Rug Journal

Pug in a Rug Journal

Pug in a Rug Journal

Hope is the pillar that holds up the world.
Hope is the dream of a waking man.

Pliny the Elder

Pug in a Rug Journal

Pug in a Rug Journal

Pug in a Rug Journal

Positive thinking is more than just a tagline. It changes the way we behave. And I firmly believe that when I am positive, it not only makes me better, but it also makes those around me better.

Harvey Mackay

Pug in a Rug Journal

Pug in a Rug Journal

Pug in a Rug Journal

Pug in a Rug Journal

Believe in yourself and stop trying to convince others.

James De La Vega

Pug in a Rug Journal

Pug in a Rug Journal

Pug in a Rug Journal

Pug in a Rug Journal

If you put enough smart people together in one space, good things happen.

Erik Hersman

Pug in a Rug Journal

Pug in a Rug Journal

Pug in a Rug Journal

Pug in a Rug Journal

Everything that is done in the world is done by hope.

Martin Luther

Pug in a Rug Journal

Pug in a Rug Journal

Pug in a Rug Journal

Pug in a Rug Journal

You begin by always expecting good things to happen.

Tom Hopkins